HEART TAKE WINGS

WINGS

Devotions in verse

STEPHANIE STRUNK BAKER

Scripture quotations in this book are taken from the King James Version of the Bible.

COVER PHOTO: taken by the author at Mill Springs Mill, Monticello, KY.

WestBow Press books may be ordered through booksellers or by contacting:

WestBow Press
A Division of Thomas Nelson & Zondervan
1663 Liberty Drive
Bloomington, IN 47403
www.westbowpress.com
1 (866) 928-1240

All photos were taken by the author with the exception of the following: eagle photos on pages 45 and 47, courtesy of Mike Hatter, photos on pages 8, 27, 30, and 32 by Roger W. Strunk, photo on page 44 by John Tyler Baker III, and photos on pages 35, 36, and 43, by Makayla M. Baker.

ISBN: 978-1-4908-3526-6 (sc)
ISBN: 978-1-4908-3527-3 (e)

Library of Congress Control Number: 2014908626

Printed in the United States of America.

WestBow Press rev. date: 05/08/2014

WESTBOW°
PRESS
A DIVISION OF THOMAS NELSON
& ZONDERVAN

Contents

THOSE TIMES WE FAIL 48

PREFACE

I want to express a special thanks to my parents, **Roger and Diana Strunk**, who believed, not just in me, but in Him who called me. Their encouragement and prayers have meant much. I started my first poetry journal at age eleven. My work needed much refinement, but they were always there to encourage me and share in my dreams. I'd also like to dedicate these musings to my own daughter, **Makayla**, who shows interest and promise in the field of writing, and my husband, **John Tyler**. These selections were all written before they came into my life, but they are a new source of inspiration.

As I worked on editing this collection, I kept recalling a comment that our Sunday School teacher, Bro. Wayne Brickner makes when he tells us some incident from his life to make a point, and I quote, *"Now this is open confession. . ."* Some poetry is putting oneself in another person's shoes, but much of it is "open confession". I hope that these poems leave a thought with you that is valuable either in your own spiritual growth, your daily life, or just for your own enjoyment.

I would like to note that the poems, *Spring Song, You Surround Us, Autumn Splendor,* and *Faith Is Essential,* first appeared in issues of the Somerset-Pulaski County News Journal in 2004. *Goodbye Summer* appeared in the Spring 1994 anthology, Poetic Voices of America and in the September 2005 issue of Kentucky Families Today. *The Daisy* appeared in the 1994 anthology, All My Tomorrows by Quill Books, and *Autumn Royalty* appeared in the July 2004 issue of Kentucky Living magazine.

Most poems are either reminiscent or deal with feelings, or are themselves prayers to God. They come from the heart and are being shared in hopes that they will touch you and inspire you to serve God, enjoy life, and make your own unique personal contribution to those that you come in contact with each day. Poetry can't be truly defined, it must be experienced, so I hope that you enjoy the following selections.

INTRODUCTION

When my thoughts are on paper
Expressed eloquently
It eases a burden
Inside of me, and
Sometimes it's just a thought in my mind
And out of curiosity
I make it a rhyme.
Sometimes a poem is written for others;
An inspiration for sisters and brothers.
Sometimes it's a prayer to my Father in heaven,
Sometimes it's a simple note of thanksgiving,
Sometimes it's a tribute, an honor, a praise,
Sometimes I write one 'cause it's one of those days.
Whatever the reason, it's written with care
In hopes that others will find comfort there.

"And, whatsoever ye do, do it heartily, as to the Lord, and not unto men;"
Colossians 3:23 KJV

THE WONDERS OF GOD'S WORLD

"O Lord, how manifold are thy works! In wisdom hast thou made them all: the earth is full of thy riches." Psalm 104:24

A MIDSUMMER THOUGHT

The butterfly on painted wing
Cannot talk or purr or sing
But as he flits here and there,
He brightens up the flowers fair.

And although he doesn't have a voice – he sings
His melody on graceful wings.
He is relaxing to the eyes
And watchers breathe contented sighs.

He is a peaceful creature and I feel that there must be
A lesson given for you and me –
Just take life slowly, gently fly
Even if you must let the world go by.

For the beautiful things aren't seen in a rush
And the most pleasant sounds are heard in the hush,
And the warm sun, gentle rain, and soft breeze
Are felt by hearts who've found their knees.

"Thou crownest the year with thy goodness." Psalm 65:11a
"He hath made every thing beautiful in his time." Ecclesiastes 3:11a
"The earth is full of the goodness of the Lord." Psalm 33:5b

THE SEASONS

How I thank God for the seasons
For I know that He had a reason
For creating Winter and Fall,
Summer and Spring – I love them all!
How dreary for it to be Winter all year long
With no sounds of life – no Spring bird's song
And how dull would be Spring each day of the year
With no hope of Summer's smile of good cheer
With no Summer sunshine – no wading the creek
No flowers blooming – no shade to seek
And how lovely the colors of Fall's golden days;
The artist tries to capture it in so many ways!
Yes, God had a plan when He made such a variety;
He knew that we humans would bore easily
So He made a mixture of seasons that blend
And offer their praises most sweetly to Him in
The warmth of the sun, the perfume of the flowers,
The breath of a breeze, the fresh air after showers,
The snow in the Winter so wonderfully white,
The stars in the sky on a clear summer night.
Yes, each season has its wonderful purpose
And the God of the seasons deserves our worship.

"To every thing there is a season, and a time to every purpose under the heaven;"
Ecclesiastes 3:1

ANNOUNCEMENTS OF SPRING

The sky is watercolor blue,
The grass is a fresh, young green,
There are little yellow dandelions,
Announcement: "It is Spring!"

I felt it long before I saw it,
For first it touched the air
And then before I knew it,
Spring was everywhere!

There's land to clear for a garden this year
But work is almost fun in the Spring
When the lilacs sweet smell is borne on the breeze
And there's beauty in everything.

The beautiful Redbuds are special this year
And the Dogwoods have on snowy white.
The picture is different each morning when I awake,
It seems like something new happens each night.

Spring is the Season that passes so fast,
Before you know it – it's gone;
But it leaves behind a wonderful change –
Sunshine, living things and a song!

"For, lo, the winter is past, the rain is over and gone; the flowers appear on the earth; the time of the singing of birds is come, and the voice of the turtle is heard in our land; the fig tree putteth forth her green figs, and the vines with the tender grape give a good smell." Song of Solomon 2:11-13a

THE DAISY

How often we ignore her
In fields where grasses grow:
The hardy little flower
With petals white as snow.

Her golden center is as bright
And cheerful as the sun.
And children pluck her
Petals slowly one by one.

I stopped to pick a blossom
And fell into her spell:
She is a symbol of the season
For she captures it so well.

She reminds me of my childhood –
When tripping through the wild,
A carefree little flower
Met a carefree little child.

She's sometimes called a "sunshine flower"
For she captures summer's glow
And she spreads a little happiness
Everywhere she goes.

So the next time you pick a daisy,
Perhaps you'll understand
What I mean when I say that
You hold summer in your hand.

"When (the fig tree's) branch is yet tender and putteth forth leaves, ye know that summer is near."
Mark 13:28b

SPRING SONG

The happiness shows on everyone's face,
A wonderful miracle – Spring is taking place!
The flowers are all budding now,
The grass is turning green.
Of all the sights I ever saw,
This one is supreme!
Everything is alive with life –
The clouds are all gone
And I'm so happy, yes I am!
And this is my Spring Song!

"All the earth shall worship thee, and shall sing unto thee; they shall sing to thy name. Selah." Psalm 66:4

SUMMER SONG

I love Summer's barefoot days,
Her laughing, carefree, cheerful ways.
I love for her to call me outdoors
As long as it is not for chores!

I love green gowns on Summer trees.
I love the light, caressing breeze.
I love the flowers brilliant blooms;
Their only fault? They fade too soon.

Birds are singing. Bees are humming.
Picnics are in – thanks for coming.
Some days are terribly hot, but I even welcome
That change from Winter's crowded, confining range.

I love the cooler Summer nights
With crickets' song and fireflies' light.
How I enjoy relaxing outdoors after work is done,
Yes, Summer is a time for fun!

"(God) gave us rain from heaven, and fruitful seasons, filling our hearts with food and gladness." Acts 14:17b

GOODBYE SUMMER

Summer, I hate to bid you goodbye
But I'll not weep, no I'll not cry.
For Autumn is coming in your place
And it's been a long time since she has shown her face.

Summer, I hate to bid you adieu
For I have grown rather fond of you.
Your days are made warm by a cheerful sun
And greeting the day has been so much fun.

But Autumn is coming; she'll be here any day
And I know you must go, though I want you to stay.
So, "Goodbye friend. I'll see you next year."
I'll enjoy Autumn while she is here.

"Thou hast set all the borders of the earth: thou hast made summer and winter." Psalm 74:17

AUTUMN ROYALTY

Summertime is clothed in greenery,
And Winter is clothed in white.
Spring is like a rainbow,
But Autumn, what a sight!

She is royalty of the seasons
As she dons her rustic robe.
She walks with regal bearing
And she is crowned in gold.

Spread about is her carpet
Of many colors on the ground.
While confetti leaves are showered,
Fall comes marching down!

"While the earth remaineth, seedtime and harvest, and cold, and heat, and summer and winter, and day and night shall not cease". Genesis 8:22

AUTUMN SPLENDOR

There's a carpet spread across the ground
Of red and gold, yellow, and brown.
The trees are clothed in bright array
Making quite a fascinating display.

And when the wind comes rustling through,
The leaves come down, more than a few!
I watch them swirling to the sky,
Then tumbling down in lullabye

And landing with the greatest ease
Upon another pile of leaves.
For this grand show there is a reason,
The welcoming of another season!

"And God said, Let there be lights in the firmament of the heaven to divide the day from the night;
and let them be for signs, and for seasons, and for days, and years:" Genesis 1:14

SNOW MAGIC

Watch the snowflakes tumble down,
Chasing, racing, to the ground.
When dark comes turn out your light;
Tomorrow, welcome a world of white.

The world is so different. How can it be?
The change came about so quietly.
A fairy-land I call it for
A new world lies outside my door.

Fascinated I could stay,
Watching nature's grand display,
I like to stay snowed in, all cozy and warm,
And look outside as icicles form.

With big, fuzzy house shoes and a nice warm fire
And a good book, to a comfy chair, I like to retire;
Just for the day, hemmed in by the snow,
Compelled by six inches to stay, not to go!

Reminds me somehow of the good old days
When things were made simple by country ways.
The best things in life are simple and kind;
But often in our hurriedness, we are somewhat blind.

I'd like to see some pure, white, wonderful snow.
I'd like to stay indoors without having to go;
So send me some snow for I want to see
Six inches of old-fashioned, fond memories.

"Praise the Lord…snow, and vapour; stormy wind fulfilling his word."
Psalm 148:7a, 8

WINTER PERSPECTIVE

There are firesides in Winter
To drive out any chill,
And I find that I love the Wintertime
When everything is still.

The pace slackens some in Winter,
It becomes a family time.
A time when we can read and talk
And I can write my rhymes.

The world rests in Wintertime;
The plants, the trees, the bears.
Winter is a resting-place
From many cares.

"As the cold of snow in the time of harvest, so is a faithful messenger to them that send him: for he refresheth the soul of his masters." Proverbs 25:13

A CHANGED ROUTINE

The trees are laden heavy
With the newly fallen snow
And even in the moonlight,
The world has a special glow.

I watch fascinated as
Snowflakes fall.
They come down fast and furious
And then there's hardly any at all.

I like to watch them pile up
Inch by inch upon the ground.
I like the quietness of the world.
Snow muffles the harsh sounds.

I love the wonder of it all.
I love the snowbound isolation –
A world away from many things
That bring us aggravation.

A world away from all the cares
Of a busy, daily life.
A little snow and a changed routine
Add a little spice.

"He giveth snow like wool." Psalm 147:16a
"Hast thou entered into the treasures of the snow? Job 38:22a

THE WIND IS HOWLING

The wind is howling
And drifts are blowing,
What a wonderful sight…
It's snowing! It's snowing!

"For (God) saith to the snow, Be thou on the earth." Job 37:6a

"For as the rain cometh down, and the snow from heaven
and returneth not thither, but watereth the earth, and maketh
it bring forth and bud, that it may give seed to the sower
and bread to the eater." Isaiah 55:10

A NIGHTTIME THANK YOU

Dear God, thank You for the lullaby
You send to me at night;
The peaceful sounds, the restful sounds
Are better than the quiet.

I hear nature's symphony in June;
All of the players are in tune.
I hear the frogs sing bass in the pond;
The whippoorwill sings songs of which I am fond.

The crickets are a mighty chorus;
I hear the hoot owl in the forest.
These all are sounds that I enjoy
Far better than a city's noise.

"The day is thine, the night also is thine: thou hast prepared the light and the sun."
Psalm 74:16
"From the rising of the sun unto the going down of the same the Lord's name is to be praised."
Psalm 113: 3

A COUNTRY GIRL

Some people love the city
And I'm frankly glad they can;
But I'm a country person
And it's hard to understand.

I couldn't trade the scenic view,
I couldn't trade the trees to you.
I couldn't trade my freedom here
For all those buildings squeezed so near.

I love the peace, the air, the quiet.
I love each country day and night.
I love to wade barefoot in streams
And dream pleasant country dreams.

Concrete and steel just don't appeal
To me right now and never will.
When I look out I like to see
God's world - not miles of industry.

Some people love the city
And I don't question their taste.
But put me in the city
And I'd be out of place.

"The earth is the Lord's and the fulness therof; the world, and they that dwell therein."
Psalm 24:1

MISS PANSY

I was introduced to Miss. Pansy
By my grandmother one fine day;
And every time I pass her now,
She has something to say.

She looks at me so earnestly
And I often see her smile.
She is such a dear, sweet thing,
So I stop and chat awhile.

Her colors are vivid
But she is not vain;
She blushes so sweetly
When kissed by the rain.

Her movements are graceful;
Her features are fine,
And pretty Miss. Pansy
Is a close friend of mine.

Now I can't stroll the garden
Without pausing to say,
"Pretty Miss. Pansy,
Have a very nice day."

And when I greet the flowers fair,
I'm reminded of how much God cares;
I know He does and I'm glad that He sent
Flowers for our enjoyment.

"[Trust] in the living God, who giveth us richly all things to enjoy."
1 Timothy 6:17b

YOU SURROUND US

God, it doesn't take a scholar
To see Your mighty hand.
We feel You in each breath we breathe;
We see Your wonders in the land.

Your love whispers all around us,
In the flowers, in the trees.
Yes, Your majesty surrounds us,
And it brings us to our knees.

Who can soak in all the beauty
And ignore the Artist's hand?
Who can bask in all these blessings
And fail to understand?

"Let all the earth fear the Lord: let all the inhabitants of the world stand in awe of him."
Psalm 33:8

18

ALL OF CREATION PRAISE HIM

Happy are the flowers
As they praise their Maker by
Lifting velvet faces
In worship to the sky.

Happy are the woodland trees
As they bend and bow to God.
Happy are the little seeds
That peek from 'neath the sod.

Happy, happy, happy,
What music to the ears!
Happiness throughout the world
To those who know that God is near.

Happy little lively brook
That ripples to the tune
Of "mighty is our Maker",
Morning, night, and noon.

Happy are the creatures
Who feel His unseen hand;
God cares for all of His creation.
Is that hard to understand?

Happy are the people
(And my heart within me sings)
Who take the time to praise Him:
The Lord of everything!

"All thy works shall praise thee, O Lord." Psalm 145:10a

THANK YOU

For rain that falls so soft and light,
For twinkling stars on cloudless nights,
For each sunset and for each sunrise,
For all of these blessings that You don't disguise,
For rainbows and the promise they hold,
For sunbeams that warm me when I am cold,
For a gentle breeze on a hot summer day,
For kindness shown in a simple way,
For bullfrogs on the pond below,
For lightening bugs' cheerful glow,
For kittens: furry, soft, and warm,
For keeping me each day from harm,
For Springtime when flowers appear,
Thank You for all things that I hold dear!

"And God saw every thing that he had made, and, behold, it was very good." Genesis 1:31a

RAINY DAYS

Oh, we like to praise the sunny days,
They make us laugh and smile,
But nothing is more pleasant
Than rain once in a while.
Rain is good for the crops and springs,
Good for flowers and all living things.

What better day is there to curl up in a chair and rest,
With a snack and the book you love the best?
What better day is there for sleeping in?
Can you think of a more pleasant way for a day to begin?
When summer is so humid and hot
A cool, rainy day just hits the spot!

"Then I will give you rain in due season, and the land shall yield her increase, and the trees of the field shall yield their fruit." Leviticus 26:4

"If the clouds be full of rain, they empty themselves upon the earth." Ecclesiastes 11:3a

HIS HANDIWORK

Dear God, You walk upon the wings of the wind;
And in Your goodness, rain You send.
You made the sun for warmth and light,
For rest, You made the dark of night.
For life, You made the season, Spring
And Winter-time, sweet rest doth bring.
And Summer, such a pleasant time!
Autumn, for a poet's rhyme?
Nothing is haphazard anywhere;
In everything, You show that You care.

"Who layeth the beams of his chambers in the waters: who maketh the clouds his chariot; who walketh upon the wings of the wind." Psalm 104:3

FROM THE HEART

"How precious also are thy thoughts unto me, O God! how great is the sum of them! If I should count them, they are more in number than the sand: when I awake, I am still with thee." Psalm 139:17 &18

HELP ME TO SERVE YOU

Lord, always keep my heart pliable and receptive to Your will.
Please help me above my hectic pace to hear it and obey it – better still.
I want You to guide this child in all that I do and say.
Help me, give me courage, and direct me when I pray.

Give me understanding when I read Your Word and sing.
Help me to put aside excessive pride and be thankful in everything.
Help me to give credit where credit is due.
I want everyone to know that what I am, I am because of You.

Help me to be more loving and forgiving.
Let others see You through me – that's my reason for living!
For You gave Your life for me so the least that I can do
Is to help others know that You love them too!

"So teach us to number our days that we may apply our hearts unto wisdom." Psalm 90:12

"Teach me to do thy will; for thou art my God: thy spirit is good; lead me into the land of uprightness." Psalm 143:10

GUIDE ME

Help me to keep my thoughts and feelings
In obedience to You;
Because I am Your child, dear God,
It's something that I must do.
All my longings, all my dreams,
I hold to them so tight,
Yet I know that I must hand them over and
Let You tell me if they're alright.
And all of the plans
That I've taken time to make,
By not asking for Your guidance,
I've made a mistake.
I have many ambitions
That are so precious to me;
But help me find in You
All security,
And not in the things that I seek to attain.
Help me in all things to glorify Your name.

"And the Lord shall guide thee continually…" Isaiah 58:11a

*"I will instruct thee and teach thee in the way which thou shalt go:
I will guide thee with mine eye."Psalm 32:8*

I WANT TO BE TRUE

Lord, I want to be a blessing;
I want to serve You well.
May the life I live for You,
Point my friends away from hell.

I want to show the children that
You are very real indeed,
And I want to help the aged
In their lonesomeness and need.

I want to help the hurting
Find sweet peace in You.
I want to serve You faithfully,
I do want to be true.

I stumble many times
And it seems
That Your plan is often
Different than my dreams.

I pray for courage to speak for You;
My own flesh fails me still.
I also pray for wisdom
So that I can discern Your will.

"Commit thy works unto the Lord, and thy thoughts shall be established." Proverbs 16:3

AFTER ALL YOU'VE DONE FOR ME

Sometimes I'm so discouraged,
Heavy hearted, beaten down;
But just when I am giving up,
You turn my world around.

I can't wallow in defeat
After all You've done for me.
And I can't waste precious time;
There's much I'm called to be.

Tomorrow is a challenge,
And a promise is today.
Yes, I can meet each disappointment
If I look at life that way.

"When my spirit was overwhelmed within me, then thou knewest my path." Psalm 142:3a

BELIEVING IN FAITH

Thank You God, that I believed,
Stepped out in faith; Your gift received,
Placed my whole life in Your hands
Although I didn't fully understand.
I know that Your Word is true;
You do just what You say that You'll do.
I still don't understand everything,
But You are my Father, my Lord, and my King.
And I've found that You bear me up when troubles 'round me roll.
Whatever happens, Lord, You have my heart and soul.
Assurance dwells now in my heart,
But I accepted in the start;
Before Your strength was proved to me,
I stepped out in faith and said, "I believe."

"That if thou shalt confess with thy mouth the Lord Jesus, and shalt believe in thine heart that God hath raised him from the dead, thou shalt be saved. For with the heart man believeth unto righteousness; and with the mouth confession is made unto salvation."
Romans 10:9 & 10

FAITH IS ESSENTIAL

Faith can move mountains,
It is said in God's Word,
And faith is essential
If we want to be heard.

Why even pray if we
Don't believe that God will send
The answer that is
Most pleasing to Him?

The answer most suitable,
For He sees the years yet to come
And He cares and He knows,
What we'll best profit from.

Sometimes faith is tested
As we spend years waiting for
The answer to the plea,
And for what God has in store.

But that's faith! Hanging on
And trusting His Word,
Knowing that He'll answer.
Knowing that He heard.

"Commit thy way unto the Lord; trust also in him; and he shall bring it to pass." Psalm 37:5
"Knowing this, that the trying of your faith worketh patience. But let patience have her perfect work, that ye may be perfect and entire, wanting nothing." James 1:3 & 4

GOD . . .

When I can't write,
You give me words.
You are the voice;
You will be heard!

And through my weakness,
You are made strong.
I am the singer, but
You are the song.

Your message will last
Through eternity;
But if I can be a blessing,
Please say it through me.

"And he said unto me, My grace is sufficient for thee: for my strength is made perfect in weakness." II Corinthians 12:9a

WILLING SERVANTS

You could force the world to follow You,
Could bend us to Your plan,
For You have power over all
That's fashioned by Your hand.

But You want humble servants
Who have listened to Your voice;
You want a world of willing ones
To follow You by choice.

You give us life for death;
You give us peace for pain.
Why some choose not to follow You,
I cannot explain.

For all we give up is our emptiness
And all we lose is strife,
Yet, You loved enough to freely offer us
Everlasting life.

And though we suffer hardships,
We are filled with peace to know
That You will always be with us
Wherever we must go.

"Have not I commanded thee? Be strong and of a good courage; be not afraid, neither be thou dismayed: for the Lord thy God is with thee whithersoever thou goest." Joshua 1:9

SOMEONE CARES

No one is "sheltered" from the cares of this life;
For we all suffer pain, and we all endure strife.
There'll be times we hurt; there'll be times we bend,
But we'll never break while depending on Him.

Trials are certain if we try to do right,
For we must combat the forces of the night.
If Christ is our Saviour, then in our life He will win,
But we face Satan's temptations to sin.

No we can't just live life with graceful ease.
We can't always be babied; we can't always be pleased.
We often stumble; the thorns are there.
But thank You, God, that You care.

"Casting all your care upon him; for he careth for you." 1 Peter 5:7

I DO, PRAISE YOU

I don't always stand before a crowd
And say Your praises right out loud,
But I am sure that my praise is heard
Through every heartfelt, written word.

Let me say in written form what I
Think of You, oh dear Lord, Most High.
In many special ways You send
Blessings without any end.

I don't deserve one gracious deed,
But You are tuned to every need
And pour out blessings by the score
That I sometimes forget to thank You for.

So this, dear God, is just to say,
Thank You for another day
Of health and home and happiness,
And family – oh how I am blessed!

And thank You that You still control
The Universe and each human soul.
You are gracious, Holy, without end;
You're my Creator and yet You are my friend!

"O magnify the Lord with me, and let us exalt his name together." Psalm 34:3
"I will praise thee, O Lord, with my whole heart; I will shew forth all thy marvellous works.
I will be glad and rejoice in thee: I will sing praise to thy name, O thou most High."
Psalm 9:1 & 2

A THANKSGIVING THOUGHT AND PRAYER

Thanksgiving comes but once a year?
Sometimes the truth of this, I fear.
For truly thankful hearts can't be confined
To designated dates or times.

Thanksgiving day I must respect;
It does give time to reflect,
And there are many who truly take the time
To exercise thankfulness in hearts and minds.

I pray, now, for a thankful heart,
May this day be just a start.
Please help me shed attitudes that hinder me
And instead pick up those that are pleasing to Thee.

And help me be thankful, God, each day of the year
For all of the blessings that I hold dear;
Not just for the big things but the little ones too,
Knowing that all blessings great or small come from You.

"It is a good thing to give thanks unto the Lord, and to sing praises unto thy name,
O most High:" Psalm 92:1

LOOK UP!

All of you who are weary,
Who don't feel the least bit cheery,
It is natural but it's sad
That cares keep us from being glad.

This is not to judge or offend you,
Or cut you down or condemn you.
Many times we've all been there –
For trials and sorrows burden us with care.

But this is just to remind you,
God will help you put hurts behind you.
His love is love with exclamation!
His love is cause for celebration!

So take the time now and renew
Your love for Him for He loves you.

"...forgetting those things which are behind, and reaching forth unto those things which are before. I press toward the mark for the prize of the high calling of God in Christ Jesus." Phillipians 3:13b & 14

SOARING IN HIS LOVE

My spirit can soar high above
Where my feet walk, Lord, in Your love.
And self-confidence is nothing at all,
But in Your love, I'm walking tall.

Nothing on my own, of that I resign,
But what I am is Your design.
And I can soar in worthy things,
For to my spirit, You give wings.

I'm not worthy for I can't be,
But my spirit lifts for You love me.
And things that get me down in life,
When worries come or pain or strife,

I'm reminded that I'm just passing through
And nothing matters, Lord, but You.
And I can't help but cheerful be
When I remember that You love me!

"But they that wait upon the Lord shall renew their strength; they shall mount up with wings as eagles; they shall run and not be weary; and they shall walk and not faint." Isaiah 40:31

GRANT ME UNDERSTANDING

Your promises I've often heard –
Lord, help me understand Your Word.
Help me to apply it daily to
The situations I go through,
For I profit most when I let You show
Me things I really need to know.
And help my mind be bright and clear
So I'll do more than merely hear.
Let me hear You speak with each word I read,
And not only listen, but give heed.

"Let my cry come near before Thee, O Lord: give me understanding according to thy word."
Psalm 119:169

THY WORD SHALL STAND

Thy Word shall stand through eternity
And someday all will bow to Thee.
Nothing is certain, nothing is sure,
Except Thy Word – it will endure.
Though all else fail and pass away,
Thy Word has found a place to stay
In my heart and in other hearts too;
Even if no one believes, Your Word still is true.

"Heaven and earth shall pass away but my words shall not pass away."
Matthew 24:35

LET GOD IN

You have a wall around you;
You think no one can get through
And you're not yielding one little bit.
You won't give in. You won't quit.
You're holding out for what it's worth,
And you don't care how much it hurts
To refuse the love God has for you.
He'll take the old – make all things new.
But you won't bend; someday you'll break.
Is heartache what it's gonna take?

Someday I pray that you will find,
Your strength is not the lasting kind.
And you'll find your weakness to be
The means for God to strengthen thee.
For in our weakness, He makes us strong.
He fills our silence with His song.
And all it takes is for us to give
In and accept, believe, confess, and live!

"….My grace is sufficient for thee: for my strength is made perfect in weakness. II Corinthians 12:9a

TOMORROW WILL COME

Yesterday has long been past;
Today is here and will not last.
We strive for tomorrow but we can't be sure
Of what it will hold; what we will endure.

But tomorrow will come; eternity's certain.
And if you're not ready, friend, you will be hurting.
So live each day with that mind.
Ask God to reign in your heart and you will find

No fear of the past – what God has forgiven,
No fear of today when for Him you're living,
No fear of the future; take each day as you receive it.
Take each minute as it comes, take His Word and believe it!

"Trust in the Lord will all thine heart; and lean not unto thine own understanding. In all thy ways acknowledge him, and he shall direct thy paths." Proverbs 3:5-6

FOR…

For blessings that You send my way,
For answering when I kneel to pray,
For strength and wisdom from above,
For light and life and Your love.
For peace that passes my knowing,
For Your hand that guides my coming and going,
For meeting me where I am with strength,
And for showing Your love to me at length.

For being there when darkness falls,
For answering when this child calls,
For all these blessings that You send,
For the loving smile of a dear friend,
For courage when I fail and fear,
For Your presence, always near.
For drying tears whenever they fall,
For being my Lord and my all.
All of these blessings I thank You for!
Each year they mean a little more.

"Blessed be the Lord, who daily loadeth us with benefits, even the God of our salvation. Selah." Psalm 68:19

THE MOST IMPORTANT THING

So many people are
Dying each day,
And too many people
Have turned You away.

So many people are
Meeting their fate!
They have made their decision by
Waiting too late.

But there are still others –
We must let them know,
That their life is in their own hands,
They can choose where they go.

Instead we let them
Wander aimlessly -
Lives that You died to
Set free.

God, it isn't that we don't care,
But why don't we take the time for prayer?
And witness in the way we walk,
And loosen up – begin to talk?

It's lives we're dealing with, we know:
The most important thing – friend's souls.

"…he which converteth the sinner from the error of his way shall save a soul from death."
James 5:20a

WHEN HE'LL CALL

Although things on earth often look so bleak,
I have thoughts on my mind and I'd like to speak.
All the good things of the past
Will endure. I know they'll last.
Things that are good and things that are kind
Cannot be changed or redefined.
Though people may go astray,
The world as a whole can't stay that way;
For if it does, the Lord is through
With things down here and will call me and you.

"…yet will I not forget thee. Behold I have graven thee upon the palms of my hands." Isaiah 49:15b & 16a

TRUSTING

We can advise and sympathize,
But when troubles hit home,
Please help us remember
Who we can lean on.

For sometimes we get down
And forget to look up.
We forget that You are our strength
And that we should trust.

Sometimes trusting isn't easy,
But the rewards are great.
You are faithful, but
We must have faith.

We can advise others
But don't let us stop there.
May we too,
Trust in Your care.

"Trust in him at all times; ye people, pour out your heart before him: God is a refuge for us. Selah."
Psalm 62:8

LESSON FROM AN EAGLE

The eagle pushes eaglets young
And flailing from the nest.
But it does no good for them
To squawk in fearful protest.

And though it seems so very cruel,
The wild things know the survival rule.
(And eaglets who never spread their wings
Are as good as dead among wild things.)

But Mama Eagle with her sharp eye
Won't let them fall and crash and die;
For she swoops down and flies below
So they won't fall until they grow

More sure, more confident of their wings
And learn the things that growing brings.
But they would never learn to fly
If they weren't ever forced to try.

So like the eagle let us grow,
Depending on no one below;
But on God, Who won't let us fall
Despite the trials that face us all.

Let us step out with faith in Him,
No matter how rough things look or grim.
For He is strong in power and might.
And we can trust that He'll do things right.

Then we won't just fly, for we can soar.
Because His strength is so much more.
Than anything we've ever known.
And His care is the greatest that has ever
been shown.

"As an eagle stirreth up her nest, fluttereth over her young, spreadeth abroad her wings, taketh them, beareth them on her wings: so the Lord did lead him." Deuteronomy 32: 11-12a

PRAISING HIM

The songs I sing to praise You,
Lift my spirit too.
It seems I get a double blessing,
Lord, by praising You.

So fill me overflowing
With this happiness I feel,
And let me convey to others
That Your love is real.

Please let me sing, if silent,
In my mind and heart,
For the joy that overflows from me
Is of praising just a start.

"I will praise thee, O Lord, with my whole heart; I will show forth all thy marvellous works.
I will be glad and rejoice in thee: I will sing praise to thy name; O thou most High."
Psalm 9:1 & 2

HEART TAKE WINGS

Heart take wings,
May cares be light,
May troubles lift
And take their flight.

May our souls dance
With joy that we
From chains of bondage
Have been set free.

Rejoice, rejoice,
Oh, why be sad?
Because He came,
We can be glad!

Oh celebrate!
We have a joy
That this world's sorrows
Can't destroy.

Oh we may weep,
But it won't last,
One day all heartaches
Will be past.

"… weeping may endure for a night, but joy cometh in the morning."
Psalm 30:5b

THOSE TIMES WE FAIL

"The Lord will perfect that which concerneth me: thy mercy, O Lord, endureth for ever: forsake not the works of thine own hands." Psalm 138:8

I WAS UNKIND

Perhaps I was unkind today,
In things I wasted time to say.
My words may have been true but I find I must bridle
My tounge, for sometimes I find it is idle.
And I must ask myself, "Did my words edify?
Did they strengthen, encourage, and glorify?"
For if they didn't show Jesus in me
Or lighten another's load, then they weren't meant to be.
And when I take the time to chatter
About things that do not matter,
Or about things that tear down, however true,
Instead of build up another or show them You;
Then I am wrong and I find
That I hurt too, when I'm unkind.

"Let every man be swift to hear; slow to speak, slow to wrath." James 1:19b

ATTITUDES SHOW

Sometimes I grumble
All day long,
And can't do right
For doing wrong.

I make others miserable
For I complain.
Why are there days
That I'm such a pain?

"A merry heart doeth good"
That I know,
And if I'm upset,
I can be sure it will show.

Why should I bring
My Saviour such shame?
For complaining and grumbling
Isn't glorifying His name.

"The Lord will perfect that which concerneth me." Psalm 138:8a
"A merry heart doeth good like a medicine." Proverbs 17:22a

BECAUSE YOU CARE

Dear God, there are many things I need
But wisdom surely takes the lead.
There are situations that I can't understand
But You know for You made humans.

So show me just what I should do,
For humanly speaking, answers are few.
Please give me compassion: a Christ-like love,
And patience which is something I'm often short of.

And give me strength if I must be strong
For others about me to lean on,
Lest I should fall - my own strength is weak,
So prop me up with Your strength, so to speak.

And give me a forgiving heart, 'til seventy times seven,
For I run short of what it takes, yet I want to be forgiven.
And help me take the pressure that others place on me,
For I can't handle stress at all without Your stability.

And help me control my anger, Lord, I lash out readily
And there are days when I complain almost constantly.
I'm loaded with faults of which You're aware
And I want forgiveness because I know You care.

"For wisdom is better than rubies; and all things
that may be desired are not to
be compared to it." Proverbs 8:11

FORGIVE ME

It's pride that drags me
down sometimes.
It's jealousy that make me blind,
And envy often
does annoy,
Depriving me of true joy.
It's unthankfulness
that makes me grumble.
It's blinded eyes
that cause me to stumble.
It's anger that makes
me lash out.
It's stubbornness
that makes me shout.
It's unbelief that
I should doubt,
And sullenness
hurts those I care about.
Selfishness makes me
want my way,
And often guides
the words I say.
Forgive me, Lord, of these
things I do
And ever let me
look to You.

"O God, thou knowest my foolishness; and my sins are not hid from thee." Psalm 69:5

ROOM TO SHINE

Torn by my pride and selfishness,
Yet humbled by Your holiness,
Often in my heart I find,
That I'm not always good and kind.
And I'm not righteous - not a bit!
And when I want to yell, "I quit!"
Then I'm reminded that I never was
Perfect nor claimed to be.
I am just what You are through me.
And a day is full of wrongs and rights
And many are the inward fights.
Please help me give You room to shine
In my life. My heart is Yours, not truly mine.

*"What doth the Lord require of thee, but to fear the Lord thy God, to walk in all his ways,
and to love him, and to serve the Lord thy God with all thy heart and with all thy soul."
Deuteronomy 10:12b*

IN ALL HONESTY

There are times at following Your leading I fail,
But You are forgiving and you know me well.
There are times I get frustrated and feel You're not leading,
But I know that's not true, I was just not heeding.

There will constantly be battles between darkness and light,
And between self, the devil, and things that are right.
I'm sure sin will continue to be attractive.
And I don't doubt that there will be times that I'm distracted,

And lose sight of the way that You're leading me.
In my human weakness, I may say, "Let me be."
But this is to thank You that I am Your child,
And that as my kind Father, You won't let me run wild.

I can't fear tomorrow; I have given it to You.
You hold my life-plans; You will see me through.
You are Lord of the future so I meet each day with delight.
For You are Jehovah, Who doeth all things right.

"In all thy ways acknowledge him and he shall direct thy paths." Proverbs 3:6

54

PLACE IN HIM YOUR TRUST

We all have our 'thorn in the flesh',
Our special trial of faithfulness.
We all have our crying time, when we shed a tear,
When we call in desperation, so that God may hear.

We all have things we think we cannot face,
But for His kindness, love and grace.
These things are in our lives I'm sure
That He might see if we can endure,

And to see if we will reach for His hand
To guide us 'round our "sinking sand".
Yes, He is faithful and to endure you must
Place in Him your deepest trust.

"Whoso trusteth in the Lord, happy is he." Proverbs 16:20b

"How excellent is thy lovingkindness O God! Therefore the children of men put their trust under the shadow of thy wings." Psalm 36:7

YOU KNOW WHEN I TRY

No one else knows
But You – how I feel inside,
And from You, dear God,
I cannot hide.

You know the things
That tempt me sore.
But You also know when
I try to serve You more.

You know when I'm angry
And when I hold a grudge.
But I am happy
That You are the judge.

For You are forgiving
When I cry, "Please forgive."
And You teach me each day
What I must know to live.

You're aware of my anger,
My selfishness too.
But You know through it all
That I truly love You.

"…the Lord seeth not as man seeth; for man looketh on the outward appearance, but the Lord looketh on the heart." I Samuel 16:7b

PRAYER FOR VIRTUES

Help me take troubles in stride,
Knowing that You are by my side.
Humanly speaking, I don't take troubles well;
Please all of my anger and bitterness quell.
And though I'm hurting, let me not take delight
In hurting another, for that is not right.
And bitterness leaves its scars on one's soul,
For it makes one selfish, withdrawn, and cold.
No, I can't let hurts and failures control me,
For then I'll never be what I'm called to be.
So don't let me grow hard with the cruel realities of this life,
But instead grow warm and cheerful and steady in strife.
Please let adversity strengthen instead of weaken me
And help me grow in wisdom, in service and in charity.

"Hear my cry, O God, attend unto my prayer. From the end of the earth, will I cry unto thee, when my heart is overwhelmed; lead me to the rock that is higher than I." Psalm 61: 1 & 2

MORE LIKE YOU

My faults are many;
My virtues are few,
But God, You live in me,
I'm depending on You

To take my weaknesses
And make me strong,
To show me my mistakes,
And to right my wrongs.

I am imperfect
And always will be
Until You in Your glory
Come for me.

But each day I strive
With Your purpose in view,
And with Your help and guidance
To be more like You.

"My grace is sufficient for thee: for my strength is made perfect in weakness."
II Corinthians 12:9a

YOU KNOW MY HEART, BUT STILL NEED TO HEAR FROM ME

You know what I need before I come to You.
You know what I need. You know when I'm blue.
You know when my joy is more than I can contain.
You know when I'm content or when I suffer some pain.
You know when I'm discontent and far, far away,
Although I desire to hear what You say.
You know all these things and yet You wait
To hear from me – why should I hesitate?
Whether I'm happy or sad it is true
That the present time is the best time to talk to You.

". . . your Father knoweth what things ye have need of, before ye ask him." Matthew 6:8b

"And in all things, whatsoever ye shall ask in prayer, believing, ye shall receive."
Matthew 21:22

"The effectual, fervent prayer of a righteous man availeth much."
James 5:16b

IN YOUR SERVICE

It didn't matter that I'd been
Apart from You and into sin;
You held out arms of love so strong –
Just said, "My child, what took so long?"

And now I see what I long knew,
I'm nothing, Lord, apart from You.
And I cannot kneel to pray
When in my heart, I run away.

You beckon me; You bid me come –
"Serve Me, My child, while you are young."
And how can I deny the cost,
Reject Your will, ignore the lost?

What can I do? What small part give?
That I might help another live?
How can I turn my back on You
When You are everything that's true?

Help me serve You while I can,
And find my place in Your plan.
Please give me words or give me music
And help me humbly, Lord, to use it.

"Remember now thy Creator in the days of thy youth."
Ecclesiastes 12:1a

LORD, YOU ARE MY EVERYTHING

You are my life; not a small part
But You are reigning in my heart.
And never though I often stray,
Can I just up and walk away.

When I wake in the morning-time,
When I sit down to write a rhyme,
When I go about my busy day,
When at bedtime, I kneel to pray.

You know my every right and wrong,
You know the rhythm of my song.
You are my life and everything
I do must be an offering.

My time, my talents aren't my own,
They're sent from You: a gracious loan.
You entrusted them to me; what can I do
But my best? Then give them back to You.

"O Lord, thou hast searched me, and known me.
Thou knowest my downsitting and mine uprising,
thou understandest my thought afar off.
Thou compassest my path and my lying down,
and art acquainted with all my ways.
For there is not a word in my tongue, but, lo,
O Lord, thou knowest it altogether." Psalm 139:1-4

STARTING OVER AGAIN

Don't let me cease to try because
Someone sees all my human flaws;
Just help me to be a light,
And all my wrongs, just make them right.

I fail You so much that I almost give up
And things that I do right never seems enough.
But then I'm reminded that none of us can ever do,
Enough in our lifetimes to ever repay You.

You expect me to serve You and do what I can,
But when failures are foremost, You understand.
You show me the right way. You lead me in love,
And Your plans are better than what I could think of.

And so I will stumble but I'll get up again,
And though You are Master and Holy, You are also friend.
You'll lead me and guide me and show me the way
I should walk and should talk and should live every day.

"For if a man think himself to be something, when he is nothing, he deceiveth himself."
Galatians 6:3

PLEASE GIVE US UNDERSTANDING

Dear God, please help Christians to gain
An understanding in Your name.
And when a brother is beset
By trials, help us not forget
That You are love. Your ways are kind.
And let prayer be the tie that binds.
We're Christians, yet we are human too
And oft do things that we shouldn't do;
Like, step on a brother when he's down
And spread an unkind word around.
And oft do things that we deem right
Regardless of how displeasing in Your sight.
And often set ourselves in a place
Of judgment on the human race,
When that is a place we shouldn't be
For inside hearts, we cannot see.
We are so hard on each other,
But shouldn't *love* be the same as *brother*?
And until we've walked a weary mile
In another's shoes, in another's trials,
Until we know the circumstance,
We cannot judge the happenstance!

". . .every idle word that men shall speak, they shall give account thereof in the day of judgment." Matthew 12:36
"Set a watch, O Lord, before my mouth; keep the door of my lips." Psalm 141:3
"Forbearing one another, and forgiving one another, if any man have a quarrel against any: even as Christ forgave you, so also do ye." Colossians 3:13

ABOUT THE AUTHOR

From an early age, Stephanie Strunk Baker has wanted to be a writer. Her first published poetry appeared in Somerset Community College's <u>Kentucky Writing</u> anthology in 1987, earning her a Certificate of Merit for outstanding work in the field of poetry writing and encouraging her dream. From there, her poetry has been published in a variety of publications, most notably in LifeWay Publications' youth magazine, <u>Event</u>, later known as <u>essential connection</u>, and their senior's magazine, <u>Mature Living</u>. Her prose has appeared in magazines such as <u>Kentucky Explorer</u>, <u>Reminisce Extra</u>, and <u>Release Ink</u>.

As an avid doll collector, she has been published in various doll collectors' magazines, most notably as a regular contributor to <u>Doll Castle News</u>, since 1996. She lives in Kentucky with her husband, daughter, and numerous pets.

Printed in the United States
By Bookmasters